Tell me...

HOW DOES MY BODY FIT TOGETHER?

...and more about the human body

CHRYSALIS CHILDREN'S BOOKS

First published in the U.K. in 2003 by Chrysalis Children's Books,
an imprint of Chrysalis Books Group PLC,
The Chrysalis Building, Bramley Road,
London W10 6SP, U.K.

This edition distributed in the U.S. by
Publishers Group West.

British Library Cataloguing in Publication Data for this book is available
from the British Library.

Every effort has been made to ensure that none of the recommended
websites in this book is linked to inappropriate material. However, due
to the nature of the Internet, the publishers regret that they cannot take
responsibility for future content of the websites.

Produced by Miles Kelly Publishing Ltd
Bardfield Centre, Great Bardfield, Essex CM7 4SL, U.K.

Editorial Director: Anne Marshall
Editor: Mark Darling
Copy Editor: Sarah Ridley
Indexer: Jane Parker
Proofreaders: Hayley Kerr, Leon Gray
Americanizer: Tracey Kelly
Designer: Michelle Cannatella
Artwork Commissioning: Bethany Walker

Editorial Director, Chrysalis Children's Books: Honor Head
Senior Editor, Chrysalis Children's Books: Rasha Elsaeed

ISBN: 1 844580 58 X

Printed in Malaysia

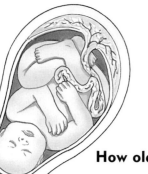

Contents

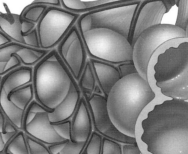

Make-its

733656

3

How old was I when I was born?

▸ A baby starts to smile from around six weeks old.

People often say that the day a baby is born is the first day of its life. But a baby does not suddenly grow by magic on this day. It has already been growing for nine months, inside its mother. Every human body begins as a tiny egg cell, as small as the period at the end of this sentence. The egg cell grows and develops in a special part of the mother's body called the womb.

placenta

a baby in the womb at seven weeks

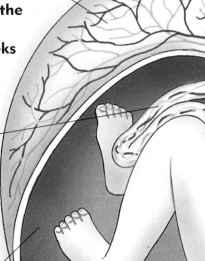

umbilical cord

fluid

at three months

bag around fluid

Bouncing babies

- Giving birth can take more than 20 hours! It is very tiring for the baby and the mother.
- More babies are born between 3 a.m. and 4 a.m. than at any other time.
- An average newborn baby weighs about 7 pounds. How much did you weigh when you were born?

at six months

nine months – ready to be born

INTERNET LINK
For information on babies
www.baby-place.com

▸ Two babies growing together in the womb are called twins.

← When did I grow fastest?

The body grows fastest at the beginning when it is a tiny egg cell in its mother's womb. In the first four weeks, it increases in size by more than one million times. If it kept growing at this rate, then by the time it became adult it would be bigger than the whole Earth!

QUICK QUIZ

1. When a mother gives birth to two babies at once, what are they called?

2. Are more baby girls or baby boys born each year?

3. How long does a new baby sleep each day?

....

Answers—see page 32.

rolling over at three to four months

↙ Why can't a newborn baby walk and talk?

A baby needs time to learn actions such as walking and talking. A newborn baby can not do much. It sleeps a lot, feeds on milk, grasps with its fingers, and cries if it is hungry, too hot, too cold, uncomfortable, or frightened.

starting to crawl at seven to eight months

cruising (walking while holding onto something) at about nine months

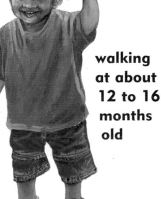

walking at about 12 to 16 months old

▲ *Most babies learn new actions in the same order. Some skip a stage, for instance, never crawling, but going straight from sitting to walking.*

5

When will I grow up?

Growth happens fast after birth. After the age of about three, growth slows down until around ten, when it speeds up again. After a time of rapid growth in the early teenage years, it starts to slow again at around 14 to 16 years. The body reaches its full height by about 19 years old. Some bodies continue to grow after this, but in weight rather than height.

▸ *By the time he is three, a child can use toys carefully.*

▲ *Toddlers from one to two years old learn holding and skilled hand movements.*

◂ *From the age of 10 or 11, girls usually start to grow faster.*

▸ *After about 16 years, growth begins to slow down.*

◂ *Boys begin to grow faster at about 12 to 13 years old.*

↓ How tall will I be?

Usually, the height of a child on its second birthday is about half the height it will be when it is grown up. A serious sickness or lack of nutritious food can slow growth, though the body often catches up later. A child with two tall parents is more likely to be taller than average. Even one tall parent increases this likelihood.

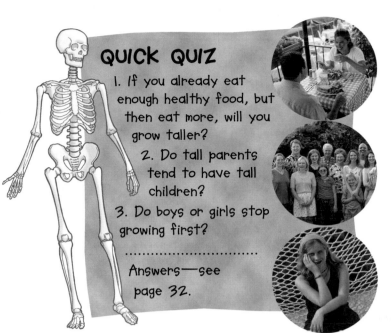

QUICK QUIZ

1. If you already eat enough healthy food, but then eat more, will you grow taller?

2. Do tall parents tend to have tall children?

3. Do boys or girls stop growing first?

....

Answers—see page 32.

Is anyone average?

You will need:
some friends who are the same age, tape measure for height, scale for weight, pen, and paper

1. Get a group together of four to six friends who are all the same age in years, and measure everybody's height and weight.

2. Add up all the heights and divide by the number of friends to find the average height. Is anyone exactly average in height?

3. Then, do the same by getting everybody to weigh themselves. Is anybody average in weight?

INTERNET LINK

Find out all about your body
www.kidshealth.org

For all the issues on teenagers and their lives
www.teengrowth.com

→ Why are we sick?

There are many different kinds of sickness. Some are caused by germs and are called infections, such as the common cold or a sore throat. Others may be due to accidents or injuries. Often, getting an sickness is just bad luck, but some are caused by lack of nutritious food or care. Young children should visit the doctor for check-ups, even if they look well, just to check that nothing is going wrong inside.

Will my skin wear off?

No! It's true that skin has to put up with a lot of wear. It gets rubbed by sponges and washcloths in the shower or bathtub, then by the towel, by clothes all day, and in bed at night. (And by fingernails when you have an itch.) However, the tough outer layer of skin is always growing to replace the bits that get rubbed off and flake.

▲ *The ridge patterns of fingertip skin are called fingerprints. They are different for everyone in the world.*

▶ *Every day, tiny flakes of skin and a few hairs fall off the body. But new ones are always growing to replace them.*

Skin deep

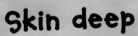

- If you could collect all the tiny flakes of skin that rub off the body over one year, they would weigh about 9 pounds!
- There are about 100,000 to 120,000 hairs on an average head.
- The thickest hairs on the body are usually the eyelashes.

⊘ How does skin feel?

Skin gives us our sense of touch and feel, because it has millions of tiny touch sensors, just under its surface. These detect objects that come into contact with the skin—if they are hot or cold, and whether they are soft or hard, wet or dry, moving or still. In fact, touch is very complicated!

QUICK QUIZ

1. Does the body have hairs only on the head?
2. What are the hairs called that lie between the eye and the forehead?
3. What are the hairs on a man's upper lip and chin called?

....

Answers—see page 32.

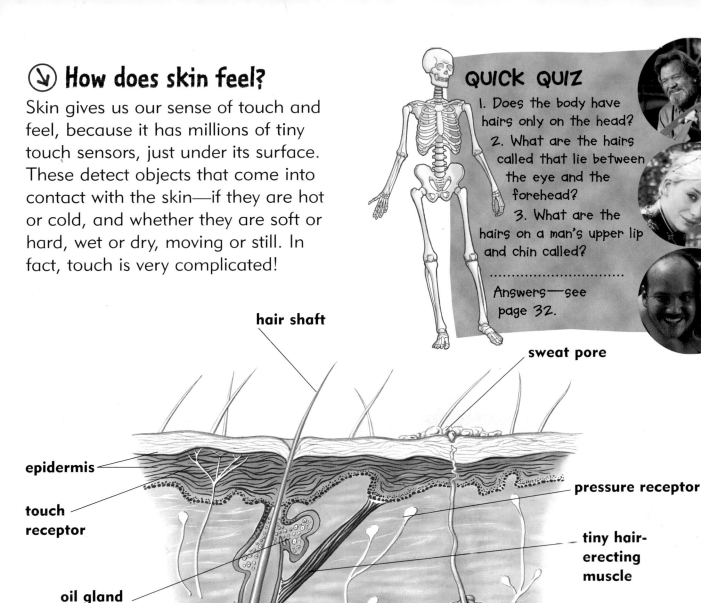

hair shaft

sweat pore

epidermis

touch receptor

pressure receptor

tiny hair-erecting muscle

oil gland

sweat gland

dermis

layer of fat

hair root

blood vessel

INTERNET LINK

All about your skin and how to protect it
www.biorap.org/br5yours.html
What to do if head lice strike!
www.bbc.co.uk/education/health/chs/headlice.shtml

⊖ Why do I have my hair cut?

To look good! Also hair would grow so long that it would be difficult to keep clean and brushed—and you might trip over it! A single head hair grows about 1/10 of an inch each week. After three or four years, it falls out. Then a new hair usually grows in its place.

9

How does my body fit together?

All your bones are connected to form your skeleton. You need your bones, otherwise the body would flop on the floor like a pile of jelly! The bones are the body's strong inner frame, to hold up soft parts like your organs, nerves, and blood vessels. They also form strong levers in the arms and legs, pulled by the muscles for movement.

skull

sternum

rib cage

humerus

radius

backbones
(vertebrae)

sacrum

pelvis

femur

INTERNET LINK

Discover all about the human skeleton
http://infozone.imcpl.org/kids_skel.htm
www4.tpgi.com.au/users/amcgann/body
/skeletal.html

patella

fibula

▸ *There are 206 bones in the whole skeleton. Each has a medical name and many have ordinary names too. For instance, the patella is usually called the kneecap.*

tibia

⊥ Are bones completely hard?

No. Some have a heavy, very hard outer layer made of a substance called compact bone. But under this is a lighter layer with lots of holes, called spongy bone. And in the center there's no bone at all. It's filled with marrow, which is soft like jelly and makes new parts for the blood.

—— **marrow**

compact bone

◀ *Inside the end, or head, of a long bone is spongy bone. It's tough and hard, but light.*

spongy bone

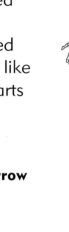

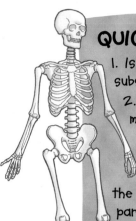

QUICK QUIZ
1. Is bone the hardest substance in the body?
2. Does a baby have more bones than a grown-up?
3. Even though bones are under the skin, do they protect parts of the body?

Answers—see page 32.

Bare bones
- The longest bone in the body is the femur, or thigh bone, in the upper leg.
- The smallest bone is the stirrup, deep in the ear—it's as big as this letter "W."
- A few people have 13 pairs of ribs, instead of 12.

▲ *The hip is a ball-and-socket design and moves many ways.*

◀ *The knee is like a door hinge, moving in only two ways.*

→ Why does my elbow bend?

The elbow bends so that you can put food into your mouth, scratch your neck, and do hundreds of other actions. The elbow is just one of the body's many joints. A joint lets the bones slide and turn and twist—without coming apart. The bone ends are covered with shiny, smooth cartilage, so that they don't rub and wear away.

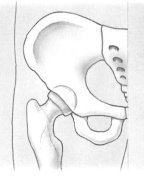

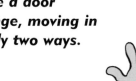

11

Why is a muscle like a piece of string?

Like string, it can pull, but it can't push. A muscle's job is to get shorter, or contract. It's connected to a bone at each end by a ropelike part called a tendon. As the muscle shortens, it pulls the bone and makes the body move. But a muscle cannot push. So another muscle on the other side of the bone moves it back again.

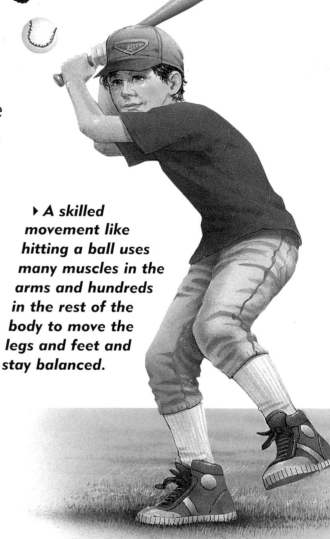

▸ *A skilled movement like hitting a ball uses many muscles in the arms and hundreds in the rest of the body to move the legs and feet and stay balanced.*

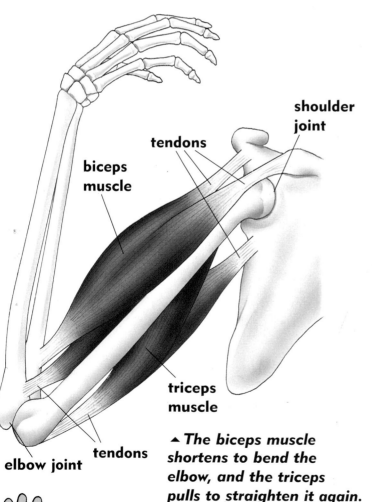

shoulder joint

tendons

biceps muscle

triceps muscle

elbow joint   tendons

▴ *The biceps muscle shortens to bend the elbow, and the triceps pulls to straighten it again.*

Muscle power

- Many of the muscles in the face are not connected to bones but to each other. You use them to make all sorts of different faces—from a grin to a grimace.
- A smile uses fewer than 20 muscles.
- A frown uses more than 40 muscles. So it's easier to smile!

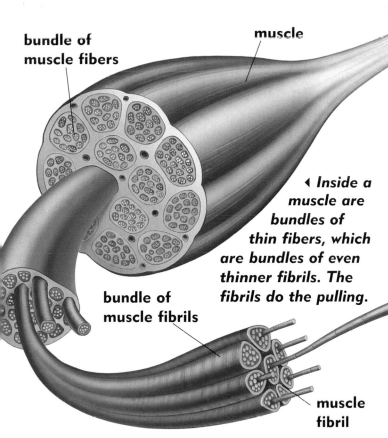

bundle of muscle fibers

muscle

◄ Inside a muscle are bundles of thin fibers, which are bundles of even thinner fibrils. The fibrils do the pulling.

bundle of muscle fibrils

muscle fibril

⬋ When do my muscles get floppy?

When you lie down, rest, relax, and sleep, most of your muscles get soft and floppy—but not all of them. The muscles in your heart keep it beating, and those in your chest keep you breathing. As soon as you lift your head, or even one finger, the muscles are working again.

INTERNET LINK
Learn about why exercise is good for you
kidshealth.org/kid/stay_healthy/fit/work_it_out.html.
Why we cough, sneeze – and other reflex actions
www.ktca.org/newtons/13/rlxes.html

Wave bye-bye!

You will need:
safe scissors, card, tape, flexible straw, thread

1. Carefully cut out a hand shape (about 4 inches across) from the card.

2. Tape the hand to the end of the straw nearest the flexible part.

3. Tape one end of the thread halfway between the hand and the flexible part.

Imagine that the thread is an arm muscle. Pull it as shown. The elbow bends and the hand waves goodbye—or is it hi?

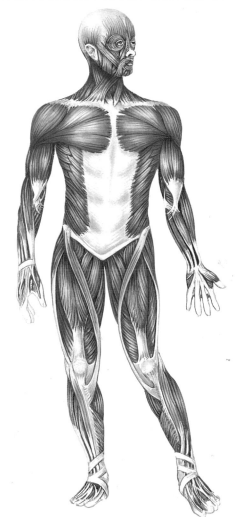

→ Could I count my muscles?

It would take a long time, since you've got more than 650! Some are just under the skin, but some are deep inside the body, so you cannot feel them. Luckily, you don't have to move each one. The brain gets used to moving whole groups of them at once, automatically.

Could I live without air?

No, the body has to keep breathing fresh air to stay alive. It only needs part of air, the oxygen, which makes up about one-fifth. Oxygen is used to get energy from food, to power thousands of processes that happen every second inside the body. The parts of the body that take in air to get oxygen are the nose, windpipe, and the lungs.

INTERNET LINK

Learn about lungs and breathing
www.biorap.org/br9/br9thelungs.html
Don't let asthma stop you having fun!
http://allergy.mcg.edu/lifequality/kac2.html

A sigh of relief

- The alveoli in your lungs are so tiny that 30 laid side by side would hardly stretch across this period.
- If all your alveoli were spread out flat, they would cover a tennis court!
- After a race, when you pant hard, you take in and give out six times more air than you do at rest.

14

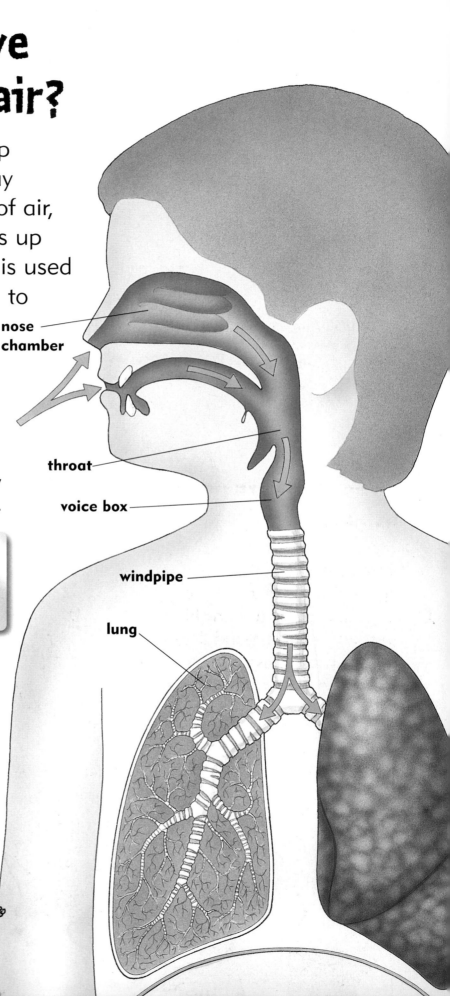

nose chamber

throat

voice box

windpipe

lung

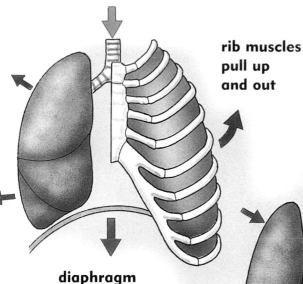

rib muscles pull up and out

diaphragm pulls down

ribs fall back

diaphragm curves back

▲ *Two sets of muscles make the lungs breathe in (above) and out (right)—the curved diaphragm under the lungs, and the rib muscles around them.*

← Do I use all the air that I breathe in?

No, you use only about one-quarter of the oxygen, which is one-twentieth of the total air breathed in. Also, the amount of air that comes out is the same as the amount that went in. This is because the body gives out a waste gas called carbon dioxide, which the lungs add to breathed-out air.

air tube (bronchiole)

→ What do I have half a billion of?

You have half a billion tiny air bubbles called alveoli deep in your lungs. Inside each one the air is very close to equally tiny blood vessels (tubes) around the alveoli. Oxygen can pass easily through the lining into the blood to be taken around the body.

blood vessels

alveoli

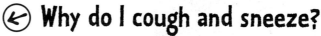

← Why do I cough and sneeze?

A cough is air rushing out from the lungs, up the windpipe and throat, and out through the mouth. A sneeze is similar, but the air comes out through the nose—at over 93 miles an hour! Both these actions help to blow out bits of dust, mucus, and other substances that clog or irritate the airways.

Could I live on candy alone?

▲ *Fruit helps your body stay healthy. It's packed with goodness, is full of juice, and tastes good!*

No, your body needs a wide variety of foods to stay healthy, especially fresh fruits and vegetables. Lean meat, fish, eggs, and milk help the body to grow at the time when it needs extra supplies of many nutrients. People who are very active need to eat plenty of energy foods, such as starches in potatoes, bread, rice, and pasta.

Food for thought

- An average person eats about half a ton of food each year, which is the weight of a family car!
- The body needs about 5½ pints of water each day.
- Most people could last for many days without food but only a day or two without water.

Why do my teeth fall out?

The body has two sets of teeth. The times when they appear vary. The first set, milk or baby teeth, usually grow from the age of about six months to three years. They fall out naturally from about six years as the adult or permanent teeth start to appear. These are bigger to fit the grown-up mouth.

3 molars
2 premolars
1 canine
2 incisors

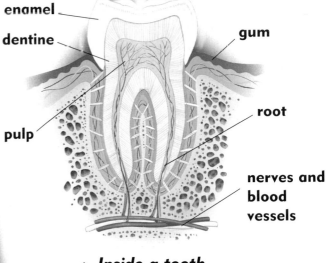

enamel
dentine
gum
pulp
root
nerves and blood vessels

▲ *Inside a tooth*

QUICK QUIZ

1. How many teeth are in the first or baby set?

2. How many teeth are in the second or adult set?

3. Which type of tooth often doesn't grow properly?

....

Answers—see page 32.

INTERNET LINK

How to make sure you have clean teeth
www.twoothtimer.com/about.htm

Fun and games on keeping your teeth healthy
www.mrreach.com

Why is the dentist my friend?

The whitish covering on your teeth, called enamel, is the hardest part of your whole body. But it must stay clean, or it turns soft, cracked, and rotten. The dentist shows you how to brush your teeth correctly, and keep your gums and whole mouth healthy. Or would you prefer toothache?

Tooth experiment

You will need:
cola drink, some dirty coins

1. Choose two old and dull-looking coins. Put one into the cola drink. Leave the other one next to it.

2. The next day, pour it out and wash the cola-coin. See how shiny it looks next to the other coin!

The chemicals have worn or dissolved the surface of the coin.

This is why it's so important to brush your teeth. You don't want them to dissolve!

Do I smell?

Yes, everyone smells—with their nose! Inside is a chamber with two hairy patches at the top. These olfactory patches detect tiny smell substances floating in air. Different hairs in each patch sense different substances, so you can detect thousands of smells, scents, and odors.

▸ *Smells give you pleasure and help to bring back memories.*

▸ *Behind the nose is a large space, called the nasal cavity. The parts that smell are in its roof.*

Smelly facts

- Our sense of smell is about 20,000 times better than our sense of taste.
- Each olfactory patch in the nose has 25 million microparts called olfactory cells, to detect smells.
- An average person can tell the difference between 10,000 different smells.

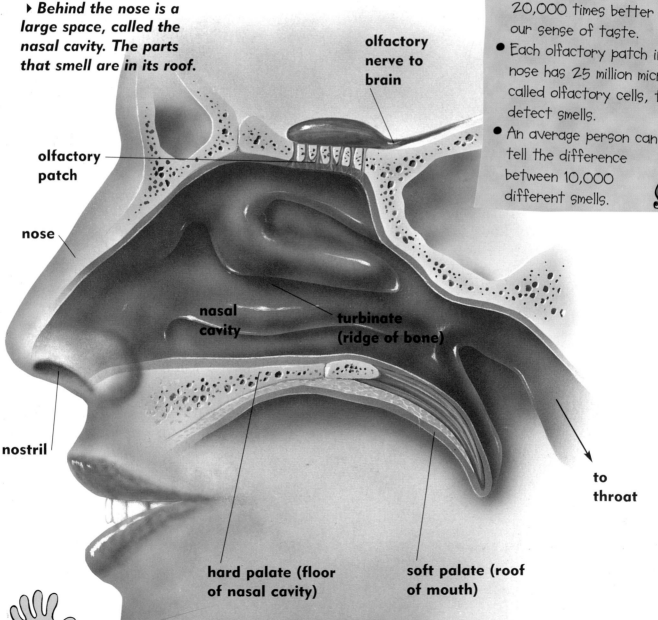

olfactory nerve to brain

olfactory patch

nose

nasal cavity

turbinate (ridge of bone)

nostril

to throat

hard palate (floor of nasal cavity)

soft palate (roof of mouth)

How many jobs does my tongue have?

It does lots of jobs, including tasting food. A terrible taste may mean that food is rotten. It helps to move food for thorough chewing. It removes bits of food from teeth. It moistens the lips so they don't dry and crack. The tongue also changes shape and position to help you speak clearly. Try to speak without moving it!

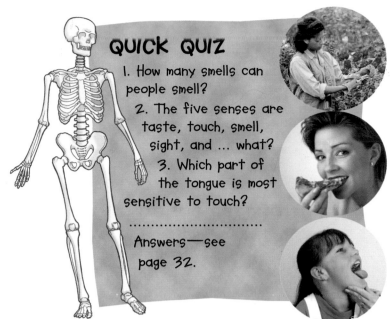

QUICK QUIZ

1. How many smells can people smell?

2. The five senses are taste, touch, smell, sight, and ... what?

3. Which part of the tongue is most sensitive to touch?

....

Answers—see page 32.

▲ **Tasting foods**

▼ **Moving foods while chewing**

▲ **Cleaning debris from teeth**

▼ **Licking lips**

▲ **Speaking**

INTERNET LINK

Why nose stuff is so yucky
http://yucky.kids.discovery.com/flash/body/yuckyst uff/snot/js.index.html

Learn more about your five senses
www4.tpgi.com.au/users/amcgann/body/senses.html

How does my tongue taste?

Your tongue is vital because it gives you your sense of taste. Tiny parts called taste buds detect substances in foods. The tip of the tongue detects sweet tastes best. The sides sense salty and sour flavors. The back of the tongue detects bitter tastes. The tongue is made up of very flexible muscles.

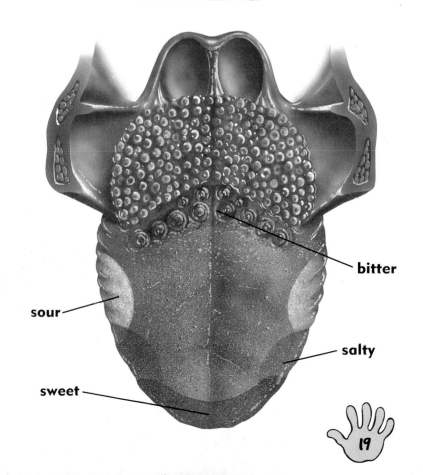

bitter

sour

salty

sweet

19

Why do my insides gurgle and rumble?

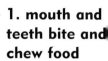

▼ *Food has a long journey through the body—it travels almost 33 feet!*

The noises are bubbles of gas inside your digestive system—the stomach and intestines (guts). These parts break down food into a mushy soup, and take the nutrients and useful substances into the body. As they add digestive juices to the food, and squeeze and squash it, gas bubbles form and gurgle along, and eventually come out at one end or the other!

1. mouth and teeth bite and chew food

2. gullet takes food to the stomach

3. stomach adds juices and churns food

4. liver stores and processes nutrients

5. pancreas makes digestive juices

6. small intestine adds more juices and takes nutrients into blood

7. large intestine takes in water and a few nutrients

8. rectum stores leftovers

9. anus lets leftovers leave body

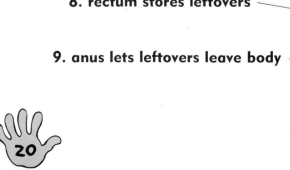

Why does leftover food turn brown?

The food leftovers that you cannot digest leave the body as brown lumps—whatever the color of the food you eat! This is because they contain substances other than leftover food. One is a substance from worn-out blood cells—bilirubin—which gives them their brown color.

QUICK QUIZ
1. Which is longer, the small or large intestine?
2. What types of food help your digestive system work best?
3. Can any foods be eaten raw?

....

Answers—see page 32.

Fast food

- Food spends 2 to 6 hours in the stomach being mashed to a pulp.
- It spends 8 to 12 hours in the small intestine.
- The leftovers stay in the large intestine for 8 to 12 hours.
- Food's total journey through the digestive system takes an average of 24 to 30 hours.

INTERNET LINK
Learn about eating and what happens to food
www.bbc.co.uk/health/kids/eating.shtml.
Find out about your kidneys and what they make
http://tqjunior.thinkquest.org/5777/urin1.htm

When is water not water?

When urine leaves the body, this is sometimes called passing water. A body system called the urinary system makes this liquid waste. Two kidneys filter blood and remove wastes and unwanted water. These pass down pipes (ureters) to be stored in the bladder, and leave the body as urine.

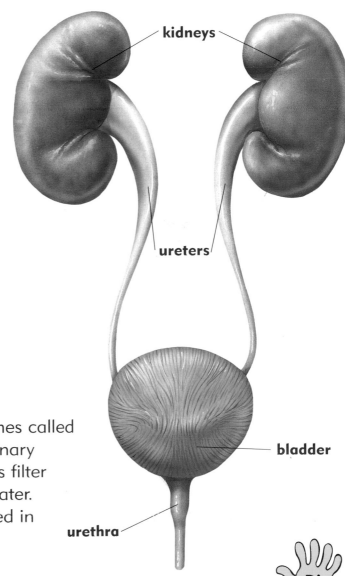

kidneys

ureters

bladder

urethra

What goes thump every second?

outer covering
muscle layer
stretchy layer
inner lining

Your heart! Every second, it squeezes hard to pump the blood inside it out through blood vessels (tubes) called arteries and around the body. The heart then relaxes and fills with more blood, coming in from vessels called veins. Then it squeezes again to pump, relaxes again to fill, and so on.

red cell

plasma
platelet

white cell

main veins from head and upper body

to right lung

to left lung

from right lung

from left lung

blood in from body veins

blood in from lungs

blood out to lungs

valve

valve

blood out to body

thick muscle in heart wall

▶ *Inside the heart are two pumps, side by side. The right pump sends blood to the lungs to collect oxygen. The left one sends it around the body.*

main vein

to lower body

Why is blood red?

It contains billions of tiny red parts called red cells. These carry vital oxygen to all body parts. Blood also has white cells, which fight germs and illness. And blood has platelets, which clump together at a cut or wound. This makes the blood turn lumpy, or clot, and seals the leak.

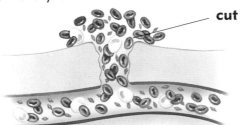

blood escapes through the cut

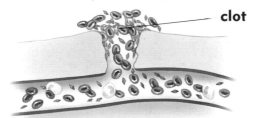

platelets get sticky and form a clot

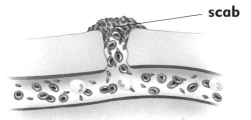

clot hardens to a scab as the wound heals

Heart to heart

- All the body's blood vessels connected in a long line would stretch three times round the Earth!
- Blood leaves the heart at a speed of 12 inches a second.
- Your heart is probably smaller than you think— about the size of your clenched fist.

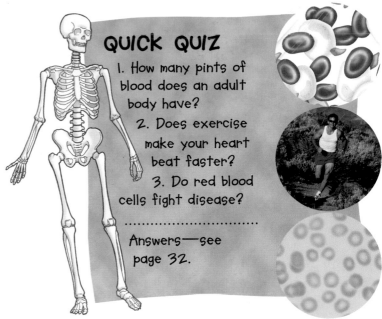

QUICK QUIZ

1. How many pints of blood does an adult body have?
2. Does exercise make your heart beat faster?
3. Do red blood cells fight disease?

....

Answers—see page 32.

Where does blood flow to?

Blood does not flow to one place and stay there. It goes around and around the network of blood vessels. The smallest vessels, called capillaries, are thinner than hairs. There are thousands in every body part. Vital substances, such as oxygen and nutrients, can seep out of them to the parts beyond.

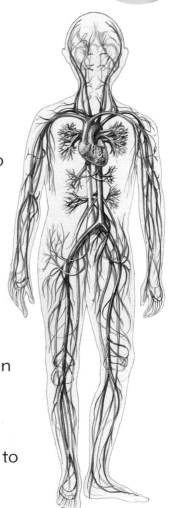

INTERNET LINK

What is blood and what does it do?
http://tqjunior.thinkquest.org/5777/cir4.htm

All about the heart and why it's so important
http://kidshealth.org/kid/body/heart_SW.html

Does the world disappear when I close my eyes?

No, it's still there. Even if you can't see things, you can hear, smell and touch them. Eyes give us our main sense—sight. Light shines through the dark-looking hole, the pupil, on the inside of the back of the eye, called the retina. This detects brightness, shapes, and colors, and sends signals to the brain, which then figures out what the eye is seeing.

▲ Eyes and ears give us lots of information about the world. Blocking these senses means we miss a lot, and may even be in danger.

◄ The eyeball is about 1 inch across. It is protected in a bowl-shaped part of the skull bone called the eye socket or orbit.

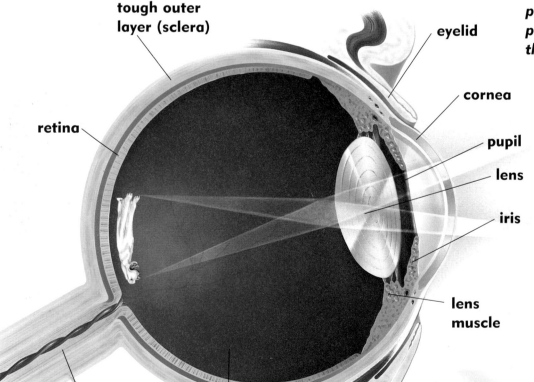

tough outer layer (sclera)

eyelid

cornea

pupil

lens

iris

retina

lens muscle

optic nerve to brain

jellylike fluid (vitreous humour)

INTERNET LINK
Find out about eyes, eye tests, and glasses
http://faculty.washington.edu/chudler/sight.html
Now hear this! All about ears and hearing
www.bbc.co.uk/health/kids/ear.shtml

⊙ Eyes can be shut—can ears?

No, ears work even when you sleep. Sounds are invisible waves in air. They pass into the hole in the ear and hit a thin piece of skin, the eardrum, making it vibrate (shake). The vibrations pass along a row of three tiny bones into a snail-shaped part called the cochlea. This detects their loudness and pitch (high or low), and sends signals to the brain, which figures out what the ear is hearing.

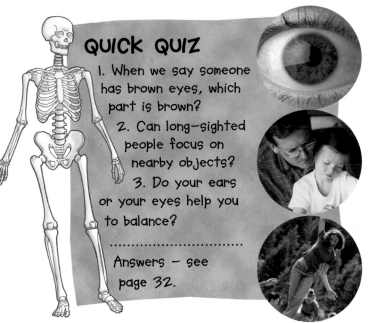

QUICK QUIZ

1. When we say someone has brown eyes, which part is brown?

2. Can long-sighted people focus on nearby objects?

3. Do your ears or your eyes help you to balance?

....

Answers – see page 32.

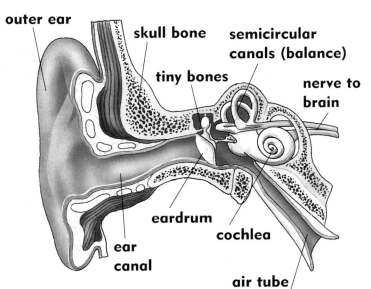

outer ear

skull bone

semicircular canals (balance)

tiny bones

nerve to brain

eardrum

cochlea

ear canal

air tube to throat

⊙ Can you believe your eyes?

Yes, usually. Sometimes we are not so sure. Optical illusions are pictures that seem to trick the eyes. Is this a vase or two people face to face? But the eyes cannot lie. They simply receive colors and patterns of light, change them into nerve signals, and send these to the brain. It's the brain that tries to make sense of the picture and in the process, fools itself.

See sharp and clear

You will need:
a small clear plastic bag (like a freezer bag), water, powerful spot-beam flashlight

1. Partly fill the bag with water. This is like the lens in the eye. It changes shape to bend or focus light rays so they form a clear, sharp picture.

2. Shine the flashlight through the water-bag on a wall just behind. Notice the shape of the beam on the wall.

3. Lower the bag onto a tabletop so it gets fatter and wider. See how the beam shape changes. The eye's lens changes shape like this to focus light rays.

▼ **Which line is longer or are they the same? The arrows confuse the brain.**

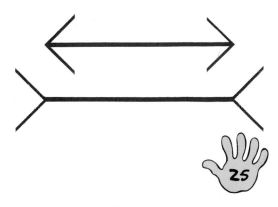

Am I very nervous?

Yes, everyone is. A huge network of nerves connect all parts of the body to the brain. They look like white string and carry tiny electrical pulses called nerve messages. Nerve messages from the eyes to the brain show what the eyes see. Nerve messages from the brain to the muscles tell them to shorten and make movements.

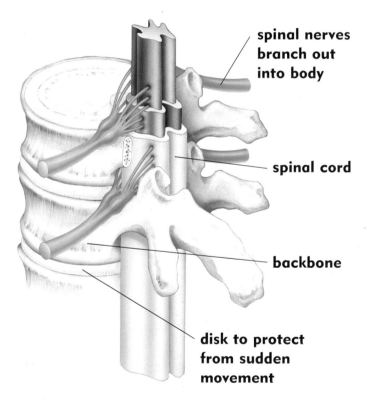

spinal nerves branch out into body

spinal cord

backbone

disk to protect from sudden movement

nerves

brain

spinal cord

sciatic nerve

▲ *The spinal cord is the main nerve from the brain down into the body. It is well protected in a tunnel inside the row of backbones.*

▸ *Nerves branch out from the brain and spinal cord to every part of the body. They carry important information between the body and the brain.*

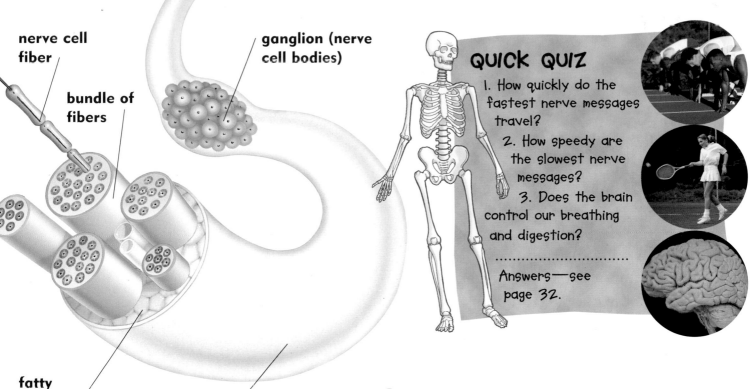

nerve cell fiber

bundle of fibers

ganglion (nerve cell bodies)

fatty padding

outer layer or sheath of nerve

QUICK QUIZ

1. How quickly do the fastest nerve messages travel?

2. How speedy are the slowest nerve messages?

3. Does the brain control our breathing and digestion?

....

Answers—see page 32.

⦿ What's inside a nerve?

A bundle of microscopic parts called nerve cells, or neurons. These are too thin to see, but some are very long, more than 3 feet! The cells pick up nerve messages at one end, carry them along, and pass them to other nerve cells, or to the brain or muscles.

Bag of nerves

- The thickest nerve (apart from the spinal cord) is the sciatic nerve in the hip and upper leg —it's as wide as a finger.
- The electrical signals for nerve messages are only $\frac{1}{10}$ of a volt. (That's $\frac{1}{15}$ the strength of a small flashlight battery.)
- All the body's nerves connected would stretch twice around the Earth.

⦿ How quick are my reactions?

A person can see an approaching ball, recognize what it is in the brain, figure out where it's going, and tell the muscles to move the arms so that the bat hits the ball—all in less than one-fifth of a second. The nervous system is designed for fast reactions to help the body avoid danger.

INTERNET LINK

Explore nerves and the brain with games
http://faculty.washington.edu/chudler/neurok.html

Loads of info on your nervous system
http://yucky.kids.discovery.com/noflash/body/pg000136.html

How do I remember?

Facts and information are stored in the brain as memories. Most scientists think memories are sets of links or connections between nerve cells. If you keep recalling a fact, like your name, this reuses the links and keeps the memory strong. If not, the links get changed and the memory fades.

▲ *You can't see inside your head, but a brain scan can. It uses invisible waves to take a picture of the brain inside the head.*

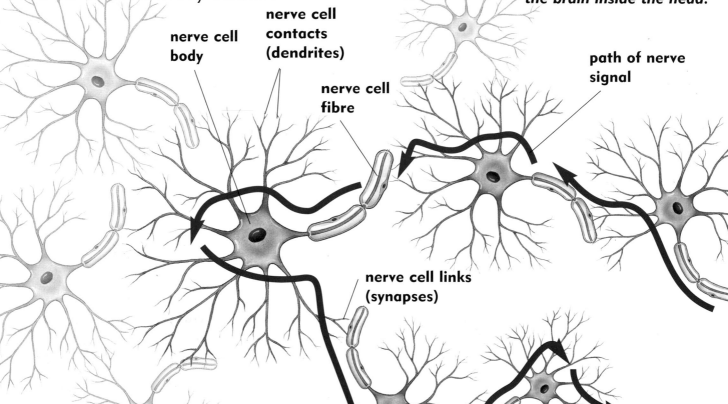

nerve cell body

nerve cell contacts (dendrites)

nerve cell fibre

path of nerve signal

nerve cell links (synapses)

Brain box

- An average brain weighs 3⅓ pounds, which is around ¹⁄₅₀ of the body's total weight.
- The brain uses up to ⅕ of all the energy absorbed into the body as food.
- The brain uses ten times more energy for its size than any other body part.

◄ *In the brain, billions of nerve cells have trillions of fibers and contacts, which make zillions of links with each other. A thought or memory may be a set of nerve signals that pass along certain pathways.*

↓ Where do I think?

Where do you think you think? Your brain is the place for all thoughts, feelings, emotions, ideas, and memories. It is a large, wrinkled, gray-pink lump, made of billions of tiny nerve cells. More nerve cells in nerves connect it to every body part. Different areas or centers on the brain's surface, its cortex, deal with different tasks.

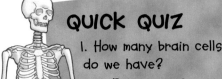

QUICK QUIZ

1. How many brain cells do we have?

2. Does your brain ever switch off?

3. What are brain scans used to detect?

....

Answers—see page 32.

movement area

touch area

taste area

hearing area

general awareness area

speech area

balance area

vision area

spinal cord

cerebellum

↓ What happens when I sleep?

Most of your body rests and relaxes, but your brain is very busy. Yet no one knows exactly what it does. It might go through the day's events, store important information as memories, and throw away other items. The brain also dreams every hour or two. If you wake during or just after a dream, you may remember it.

▼ *Most adults need between 7 and 8½ hours of sleep every night, but as we get older, we usually need less and less sleep.*

INTERNET LINK

Learn more about your brain and what it does
http://home.san.rr.com/ed4u/documents/
humanbody/page4.html
Loads of brain stuff and links
http://kidshealth.org/kid/body/brain_SW.html

29

Are my genes blue?

You may have some blue jeans to wear, but your body's genes are not colored. Genes are sections of chemicals that are too small to see except under a powerful microscope. The chemicals are called DNA (deoxyribonucleic acid). Genes are instructions for how the body grows, develops, and performs its life processes. Every tiny cell in the body has a set of them.

▶ *The twisted chemical DNA makes up genes.*

cell membrane (outer layer)

folded sheets or membranes inside cell

control center of cell (nucleus)

◀ *The body is made of microscopic cells, and every cell contains genes, as well as many other tiny parts.*

INTERNET LINK
What is a gene?
www.kidshealth.org/kid/talk/qa/what_is_gene.html

⟲ Where do genes come from?

From parents. When a baby begins as a tiny egg-cell, it receives one set of genes from its mother and another set from its father. Genes carry many instructions, such as how tall the person will be, whether they will be male or female, and the color of the hair, eyes, and skin. This is why a child inherits different features and looks similar to its parents. It is also why brothers and sisters may look alike.

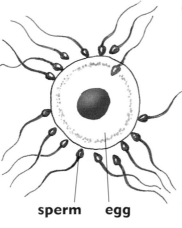

sperm   egg

▲ **Only one sperm cell can join the egg cell to make a new human being.**

QUICK QUIZ

1. Is the full set of genes for the body called the genime, genome, or genume?

2. Do my genes control the colour of my eyes?

3. Do my genes control the length of my hair?

....

Answers—see page 32.

In your genes

- Most cells in the body are less than .0008 inches across.
- There are 35,000 to 40,000 genes in each cell.
- All the DNA in one cell straightened and joined would stretch over 20 inches.

Make a new person!

You will need:
card, colored pens, safe scissors

1. Carefully cut out two head shapes from card, with ears, hair, chin, and neck. Make them the same size and shape.

2. One is the mother. Draw and color her hair, eyes, nose, mouth, and other facial features.

3. The other is the father. Give him different hair, eyes, and so on.

3. Their child would receive or inherit features from each parent. Cut out different parts of the two heads, and put them together to make a new face. Can you see the similarities?

→ How big are genes?

Very, very, very small. If you could take all the information that genes contain in chemical form, and change it into words, then you would fill more than half a million books like this one. Yet all the genes are packed into each body cell, which is 100 times smaller than this period.

Index

Quick Quiz answers

Page 5
1. Twins
2. Baby boys
3. About 20 hours out of 24, although this varies

Page 7
1. No
2. Yes
3. Girls

Page 9
1. No
2. Eyebrows
3. A moustache and a beard

Page 11
1. No, the enamel on teeth is harder
2. Yes, a newborn baby has more than 350 separate bones. But some of these join during growth. An adult usually has 206 bones
3. Yes, the ribs form a strong cage around the heart and lungs. The skull forms a hard case around the brain

Page 17
1. 20
2. 32

3. In some people, the wisdom teeth at the back of the mouth never appear

Page 19
1. More than 10,000
2. Hearing
3. The tip

Page 21
1. The small intestine
2. Fruit, vegetables, and cereals
3. Yes, most fruits and many vegetables, and even fish, such as Japanese sushi

Page 23
1. Five
2. Yes
3. No, they carry oxygen

Page 25
1. The iris
2. No
3. Both

Page 27
1. More than 330 feet a second
2. Around 3 feet a second
3. Yes

Page 29
1. Up to 100 billion neurons and even more supporting cells
2. No
3. Disorders and damage to the brain

Page 31
1. The human genome
2. Yes
3. No